Chapters

CW00392419

Dedications

Firstly, I would like to thank my parents for their support not only during that year off, also through my entire life, without that, this book would never have been possible. Most of all I would like to dedicate this book to my son William, who I hope will read this one day, then go on to make his own dreams a reality.

A bird sitting on a tree is never afraid of the branch breaking, because his trust is not in the branch but his own wings. Believe in yourself.

Beginnings

Dreams are a succession of images, emotions and ideas that occur in the mind during sleep.

I honestly cannot recall having a dream in which I took a year off and did nothing else but fish, however the idea had been floating around my mind for some time and it was something I wished I could pursue at some stage in my life. So, as I disembarked the bus and lumbered my way along the grey, wet leaf strewn pavement that lead to the building of my employment, my only thoughts, instead of my duties that awaited me, were once again turned to catching big fish and experiencing new exciting venues.

It was February 2004 and as I flicked through the pages of a client's file I kept telling myself I need to make more time to go fishing. Every time I gazed through my office window I would assess the fishing conditions, warm summer mornings would evoke memories of catching plump tench from a lilly fringed pond, mild overcast winter evenings I would be contemplating landing a big river roach and if a strong south westerly blew up, I could envisage myself holding a stunning mirror carp. All but a dream, as I turned my attention back to work, I would be confined to occasional weekends and a few holidays to improve on my big fish list – or would I?

My job at the time was just that, a job, not a career, not something that excited me so much that I felt I wanted to do it until my bus pass was issued! It could have been any job. I was in the mortgage business and had become tired of swapping clients to new deals and searching for the lowest interest rate.

Every anglers dream would be to go fishing in perfect conditions. A rising river for barbel, a strong south westerly when bivvied up on a gravel pit or fishing for pike during a "fry frenzy!" Like the majority of weekend anglers, every time that south westerly blew, I was in a meeting, when the river did rise I was confined to the office, then come the weekend, the wind would change, the river would drop and so would your chances of catching a PB! These are the challenges that the average angler, like myself, faces and as with any hobby the more time you can dedicate to it, the better you can become and the more chances come your way.

12 months previous I had applied to join a couple of famous syndicate venues, one being Linear Guys complex and the other Horton Boat Pool, both steeped in history with a track record for big fish. I would have been happy with one of those offering me a ticket, however, upon enquiring at the respective offices both venues informed me that I would be offered a ticket in the coming Spring. Brilliant, what a result. My biggest problem would be how to get the best out of the venues with only having limited time available and the distances in which I had to travel to reach them was significant.

I suddenly realised I had a once in a lifetime opportunity, I was in my 20s, single, living with parents and with very little out goings, I yearned for more time chasing big fish, to be dedicated to fishing albeit for a short term, I yearned for an adventure. I was determined to save as much money as possible over the coming months, then I would hand my notice in and start my adventure in the spring, dedicated to fishing. It sounds reckless however sometimes you have to go with your heart.

I sacrificed nights out at the weekends, instead of buying a new shirt I bought bait, I invested in hooks, swivels and bits and bobs that would see me through the many months ahead. I saved as much money as I could afford even landing an evening job so I could save a bit more cash. Suddenly everything was coming together, money was being saved, I had my syndicate tickets on their way and gratefully the understanding of my parents who realised I would be on the bank at least 5 nights a week so would not be eating them out of house and home for the next 12 months.

When embarking on any adventure whether it is setting up a new business, walking the Alps or my case fishing for a year, support from your family is essential. Their support gives you the peace of mind you require, leaving you to apply your focus on the goals you set out to achieve when you chose to start a lifetime opportunity and I cannot thank my family enough for their encouragement, also the odd pack of bacon and tin of beans were gratefully received.

It was an incredible experience that truly was a once in a lifetime opportunity, here is my story....

Tench – Off to a Flyer

I had decided to begin my campaign on Horton Boat Pool in Berkshire part of the CEMEX Complex (now disbanded) it is a secluded mature lake which is primarily a catfish venue with fish over 70lb. However, it was the quality tench and bream that attracted me along with the odd carp that swam within the water. As the bailiff approached, I walked the thoroughly laden barrow to my chosen swim. He was a forlorn, gaunt figure resembling Catweasel with his whiskered face, several ear piercings and a threadbare jumper, his story was one of obsession.

I was familiar with the bailiff, as I had recently walked the banks on a recce and spent a few hours talking to the other members on the annual open night just a few weeks previous. It all started for him in the 1990's when he first fished the Boat Pool, the first time he hooked a catfish was a day he never forgot, the fishes fighting qualities were a thrill, a real adrenalin rush which soon became an obsession. At first, he would spend every weekend at the lake, then he would use all his holiday entitlement to fish even more, he rapidly spent less time at home and when work got in the way of his fishing he packed that in, eventually spending all year living in his bivvy on the banks, in the colder months he would angle for the carp with some success. Over the years he was made a bailiff even had a swim named after him and to this day is now the head bailiff carrying out a splendid job of rearing the Horton carp of the future.

Due to the size of the catfish available and the superb fight they gave a lot of regulars would find it strange I would be targeting the other species however along with Vince they were a friendly bunch and always gave advice whatever you decided to fish for. I chatted with the bailiff for 10 minutes and ironically decided to fish in a swim called "Vince's" a swim in the corner nearest to the church pool. It was a quiet corner of the lake due to the Church Pool still adhering to the original close season. To my left was a reed lined bank, open water in front of me and a lovely bay area with an overhanging tree to my right, it was a popular swim, however being a Monday morning there was only one other angler on the lake.

Having 2 rod licences meant I had the opportunity to fish up to 3 rods however in some swims more rods will mean less bites and can cause problems when landing fish. I decided 2 rods would be sufficient in this case due to the confined nature of the swim. I would rather catch fish on fewer rods than no fish on 3 rods! My tactics were going to be mass baiting with particles and broken boilies fishing Maple8 boilie on the hook, I was soon to find out how much the resident tench and bream adored this flavour. I made several casts with the marker rod to get an idea of the complexion of the swim and found a decent depth along the reed lined margin. I planned to bait the margin up during the day and fish it in the evenings until the following morning and repeat each day, hoping to catch mainly tench from this area. A baiting spoon and an extending pole was used to bait the margin spot with several liberal helpings of particle mix which I cooked myself over a series of days prior to fishing. It included maple peas, maize, hemp, wheat, broken boilies, liquid molasses and some ground bait to bind it. I had kilos of this mix in several buckets in the van, I did not intend to hold back. It was now the middle of May, it was warm and with the fish preparing to spawn in the coming month or so, they should be looking to pile on the pounds in preparation for this annual event.

The marker lead revealed a second spot, a clear area the size of a snooker table about 45 yards out with patches of weed surrounding it. I intended to one rod here and if the margin rod did not produce within a couple of days I would put that on here for the duration of my 5-day stint. Both rods were fished with captive back leads, essential so as not to get in a tangle in the darkness of night when playing a fish and also to conceal the line laying along the margin. The rules on the venue meant you could fish for a maximum number of 5 consecutive days and are not able to return for a further 48 hours. That rule suited me, I would fish hard for 5 days then back home for a few pints and stock up on bait then head back out.

I set about the task of baiting up, a spod was used for the open swim, I cast the empty spod out at first to the distance required then clipped the line up on the spool which would mean baiting up as accurately as possible as I only had a small area to aim for. I initially put out 8 kilos on this open spot which took some time and a further 2 kilos in the margin spot which was relatively easy compared to the constant casting the heavy spod! Using a spod means you can mass bait a concentrated area in a short space of time, although specialist tackle is required to be as accurate as possible. Specialist spod rods are on the market, used ideally in conjunction with a big pit reel. I prefer to use a leader made of braid of a very strong breaking strain to take the initial impact of the spod over multiple casts with a lighter line to give a greater distance.

My rigs when fishing for tench, bream and carp are very straight forward on gravel pits unless I require a specialist rig in a certain situation, so unless otherwise stated my first choice at the time was an inline lead, normally 3oz, braid hook length 4-6 inches tied knotless knot style. My only addition nowadays is a piece of shrink tube curved over the eye to help with the hook hold.

It was now mid-afternoon, both rods were cast out to the baited area and it became overcast and looked like the possibility of rain. I equipped the bivvy with its second skin to offer more protection against the elements. The kettle boiled and I soon had a cuppa in my hand as the rashers of bacon sizzled in the pan. There must be no better smell when on the bank than the smell of sizzling bacon, it still evokes memories today of all those early morning breakfasts I enjoyed whilst pursuing big fish. It's a satisfying sandwich when accompanied with brown sauce.

One of my first tasks on any new venue is to draw a bird's eye map of the lake marking any significant areas of interest, e.g. reed beds, over hanging trees and shallow or deep areas. I also use a compass to identify North East, South and West even with the onset of technology, Google Earth is a useful tool however I still prefer to draw a map of any new venue as I feel this gives you a more intimate knowledge. I try and use the marker rod only once in any swim, making a note of any underwater features on my map throughout the season, if I then return the same swim I can refer to my notes and the marker rod doesn't have to make an appearance and you can start fishing straight away, especially if fish are in the area you will not disturb them by casting a marker float around their heads.

With the venue only a stone's throw away from Heathrow Airport your day is accompanied with the sound of aircraft engines as the planes prepare to land and take off from one the busiest airports in the world. Although this doesn't sound idyllic, you soon become accustomed to the noise and take an interest in them when the fish are not biting. As I gazed skyward, the bite alarm let out a bleep as I quickly turned to face my rods. The bite alarm drowned out the sound of the jet engine as the fish took off and the bobbin soared upwards seeing me rush to pick up the rod and connect with my first Boat Pool fish.

As I played the fish I was not certain what it was as was the array of species in the lake. The fight was strong as it buried itself in a weed bed. I kept the pressure on the fish as it came towards the bank it attempted to escape in the reed lined margin, I then saw the fish, a fine looking tench and a big one at that! When an angler realises he is connected to a possible personal best its heart in the mouth stuff, all his thoughts and prayers go into landing that fish, all sorts of deals are done with the devil, I kept repeating "please stay on, please stay on" thankfully the tench did stay on and my run of luck started there with that single fish. As it lay on the unhooking mat I knew it was a PB, a strong looking tench with vivid red eyes and pronounced fins.

The tench was safely in the sling as I hoisted it from the unhooking mat, the needle went to 7lb 11oz. I lowered the fish and raised it again, same result 7lb 11oz. What a start it was a new PB by over a pound. Unfortunately, the photos do not do the fish justice, the digital revolution was fairly new and although I had heard of digital cameras I did not own one. My camera had no self-take option so I had to settle for a mat shot as there was no other anglers nearby. I could not have asked for a better start.

As I took in what had happened, first cast, first bite resulting in a big tench the same rod went again, this time no warning bleeps just a scream of bleeps as the fish took off with my baited hook. The fight was similar to the first, I guessed it may well be another tench and I was enjoying my first couple of hours into my yearlong campaign. As I netted the tench it looked of similar size to the first, however on the unhooking mat if looked fatter, certainly lighter in colour with a tail fin big enough to power a barge!

The second tench took the needle to 7lb 14oz, I had beaten my PB twice within 45 minutes, talk about off to a flyer I could not have dreamed of a better start. With 2 fish being caught so early into my session I topped up the swim with a further 12 spods of particle mix and a couple handful of boilies to keep the fish interested in the area. It was now early evening and I prepared for the nights fishing ahead of me, I was full of hope after the great start and during the night I landed several bream to 8lb from both the margin spot and the open area. I did not manage much sleep that night however that was the last thing on my mind, my purpose was to catch fish and I added another tench at first light on the margin rod around 6lb. The fishing was incredible, I felt I had got my tactics right and the fish were responding to the mass baiting approach, surely it was only a matter of time before the carp moved in!

Early that morning, just as I was devouring the last of a bacon sarnie, Vince popped by to see how I was getting on. "Any Cats?" he enquired, as sometimes the catfish will pick up boilies intended for another species.

"Not yet" I replied, "Loads of bream and a couple of quality tench though" feeling satisfied with my fishing so far. Vince then went on to explain that Martin Bowler was due at the water today as he was writing a feature for Angling Times on float fishing for tench. To an aspiring specimen hunter like me Martin Bowler was becoming a legend, once the holder of 2 British records and regular features in the angling press; he had accomplished what most anglers only dream about, earning a living from fishing. I joked with Vince that if he needed any advice then point him in my direction!

I spent the rest of the morning topping up the swims with more bait via the spod and baiting spoon and also replaced my rigs after the hectic nights fishing. The sky was cloudy with a hint of blue, the rain that had threatened yesterday did not materialise and as another jet engine roared above preparing its landing gear a car pulled into the carp park. A long-haired figure sporting a baseball cap emerged making his way to the gate, this could only be Mr Bowler. He made a quick recce of the lake and as he approached, I greeted him good morning. He asked how my fishing had been so far and congratulated me on my PB tench and explained he was writing a feature for Angling Times. He had intended to fish the reed lined bank to my left as he was float fishing with a centrepin he would not require to cast far. I pointed out my baited area and he agreed to fish a little further down so as not to intrude. We then spoke about carp and chub fishing for a while before he departed to set up his float rod. For the next couple of hours, the fishing was a little slower, I noticed Martin had landed at least one fish, which he slipped into a large keep net he had special permission to use as he intended to photograph his catch at the end of his session.

As I sat on my bed chair contemplating whether I should top the swims up, the bobbing danced below the rod, jumping up and down before the line pulled solid and the rod tip shook. Due to the fact it was not a screaming take I presumed it must be a bream, I struck the rod and felt a heavy resistance, if it was a bream it was going to be a big one!

The fight was a strange one. The fish felt heavy although there were no powerful runs, no shaking of the head just a plodding reluctance at being reeled in. As the fish drew near I still thought I had hooked a very big bream which I would have been delighted with, I then caught sight of it below the surface. It was a grass carp and not a bad one, certainly a double, I easily netted the fish then all hell broke loose! In the net the carp thrashed and kicked the water to a foam, I left it in the water for a few minutes before putting it on the unhooking mat so as not to cause the fish any damage. As usual there were no other fisherman to take a picture for me, I just had to invest in a self-take camera! I looked up to see Martin playing a fish and I didn't want to leave the carp on the mat for any unreasonable length of time. It was a mid-double not a PB so I decided to slip her back.

As the evening drew close, Martin approached and asked if I would kindly do the honours with the camera instead of him relying on self-take shots (I wish I had asked him to photograph that grassie now!) obviously, I agreed and we strolled towards his swim. Within the keep net were a brace of tench in the 6lb bracket and 3 bream up to 7lb all caught on the float. He showed me how to focus on what was obviously an expensive piece of kit as he held up the tench and laid the bream in front of him as I took several shots from different angles. The feature was going to be printed within the next month, he could not give me an exact date and as I was fishing during the week I never managed to buy a copy of the Angling Times that would have seen the photos I took used within it. As a thank you Martin gave me 3 kilos of a new Dynamite bait that was due out, Marine Halibut, which has gone on to catch loads of big fish since.

The sky suddenly became very overcast and on returning to my swim I got to work spodding out a kilo of the halibut boilies followed by several spods of particles before nightfall. With the darkness came a prolonged downpour, this was certainly overdue. Although I managed a few bream during the night the fishing had become reticent due to the conditions, which left a puddle in the doorway to my bivvy! It was now my third day on the lake and although overcast remained dry and mild with a gentle breeze, ideal conditions for catching fish.

My tea was far too hot to drink as I blew into the cup to cool its contents. I opened my diary so I could update it with the night's events as I did each morning. Not a great deal to write about apart from receiving a soaking during the downpour whilst landing those bream that decided to feed in the atrocious conditions. Both rods were now on their baited areas lying in wait for a passing fish to show and an interest in my Maple8 hook baits. I stood up to scan the lake for any signs of fish that might be showing as I took another sip of tea. There would be no mistaking the next bite as the alarm went into melt down screaming it's tune.

The rod arched over as I lifted it off the rest, no need to strike, this fish was hooked and was going at a rate of knots towards the middle of the lake. The fish pulled away and I had to fight for every inch of line, this was no tench! The fish was heading to my right into the bay area. There was a tree between me and the bay, this meant that if the fish found sanctuary in the bay I would have to play it back around the tree, a difficult proposition. As the fish headed ever further to my right it was inevitable that it found its way into the snaggy bay with its overhanging trees. I prayed my size 10 hook would hold as I held the rod out at arm's length around the tree with the line at right angles as the fish splashed and tail slapped the surface. I could now see it was a very pretty mirror carp. Question was now – could I land the fish? I played the fish inch by inch away from the overhanging branches, eventually getting her in front of me where her fight was not over, only a few minutes later when she was safely in the mesh of the landing net, I gazed at my prize.

I hoisted her onto the unhooking mat, she was a fat mirror with a beautiful pink and orange colouring to her belly and a thick dark back, a stunning looking fish. Luckily a passing angler agreed to help with the photos and he snapped away as I held her up. He recognised her as a fish called Penny. She sent the scales around to a few ounces over the magical 20lb barrier. I was over the moon, what a start to my campaign, I was off to a flyer!

Bream – My Run Continues

Following the success of my latest session, I just had to return as soon as possible, so within a few days, this time accompanied by my Dad we were back on the banks of the glorious Boat Pool. On arrival, as always, we took a stroll around the lake and discovered the swim I fished on my previous session (Vince's) was taken along with a couple more along the same bank. We decided to fish from the top end of the lake, no anglers were there at present, the neighbouring swims we chose to fish both had margin features along with a wealth of open water to target, ideal for the bream and carp.

When the Old Man and I fish together, especially when in adjacent swims we tend to fish as a team instead of two separate anglers. In this case we decided to use a mass baiting approach with particles however instead of baiting 2 separate areas, we would spod a large area in between our swims and both fish rods on or near to this area to maximise our chances. Our other rods would then be fished to our own marginal features. As the weather forecast wasn't ideal, cloudy with spells of heavy rain, we got to work setting up the bivvies' before putting the rods out. I was nominated with the arduous task of spodding and proceeded to spod several kilos of particle mix over a large area that we could both cast to. As far as hook baits were concerned I was going to edge my bets and fish maple8 on one rod and maize on the other.

The bay to my left had a plethora of carpy features. Margins bordered with reeds; overhanging trees with their branches embracing the clear water; it also boasted a healthy patch of lily pads. It provided me with the dilemma of which one do I target. I enjoy the challenge of close range fishing and a certain amount of patience is normally required, so after careful observation I decided to fish on the edge of the lillies and back lead so as to keep the line as discreet as possible. It started to spit with rain as we enjoyed a bacon sarnie which was slowly becoming my staple diet on these sessions. The evening drew in as we prepared for a potentially dank night.

It rained periodically throughout the night, with the alarms giving the occasional bleep but never materialising into a run. The day passed, by mid-afternoon it was raining steadily. It felt cold today, not ideal conditions for catching fish. I zipped up my fleece jacket to keep the chill out, then suddenly the Old man's alarm sounded with the bobbin shooting up to the rod, which lead him to make a controlled strike and he was soon playing our first fish of the session. It was a spirited fight and I readied the net as a pristine roach slipped over the cord. The roach was just short of the magical 2lb barrier and the Old Man was delighted with the fish as it was certainly his PB.

I took a few photos as the rain came down, unfortunately due to the dull conditions and low quality of the camera they did not come out well enough to do the fish any justice, the roach that took a liking to flavoured maize was soon slipped back. The fish had lifted our spirits on what was a miserable afternoon and I topped up the swims with more particles. We were concerned no bream had showed over our baited areas yet and the fishing was subdued to say the least for the first 24 hours. The weather wasn't helping as it stayed cool and wet. The rain eventually eased off during the evening and we chatted before retiring to our respective bivvies'. Due to the thick cloud cover the night felt heavy and darker than it should have been. It remained dry during the night and just after midnight the Old Man received another take, this time as he lifted into the fish the rod established a healthy curve and as he played the fish commented that it felt like a sack of potatoes. Surely this must be a bream, in the dim torch light we noticed a large back and dorsal fin break the surface. The fish wallowed in the darkness and we could make out a huge bream, certainly the biggest I've seen in the flesh. I netted the fish and congratulated Dad instantly, I just knew it was going to be another PB for him.

The scales confirmed what I already knew as they read 11lb 10oz, a PB. Two euphoric anglers in the darkness, one holding a double figure bream as the other photographed the occasion. Landing a double figure bream was one of the reasons we joined the Boat Pool and it was a stunning looking fish as we retired to our bivvies' happy. I remained bite less until the following morning when the margin rod resulted in a tench in the 5lb bracket. Being our final day, I decided to change hook baits on both rods and fished them both over the particles in the hope it may bring me a change in fortune.

I attached a top banana boilie to both rods and cast one slightly beyond the spodded area in case any fish were feeding on the edges. The day remained dull, overcast and uneventful until mid-afternoon when the bobbin on the newly cast banana boilie rod shot up to the blank and remained there with the line pulling tight but not screaming off. As I lifted the rod my thoughts were of a small tench or roach however when I struck into the fish the heavy resistance revealed the culprit was certainly a bream. I would of much preferred to of caught the bream on a lighter rod however due to the big cats that reside in the lake, carp rods had to be employed to give us a chance if one did by chance pick up our boilies. The bream sailed to my left using its broad shape to its advantage, however I soon had the fish near the bank and thoughts of a double raced through my mind. It was not to be however at 9lb 8oz it was another PB. My aim when I started on this adventure was to improve on my personal best list and I was certainly doing this in the first few weeks. I returned from the venue very happy and it would not be long before I was on the bank again.

Green & Gold – The Old Man Strikes a Double

My next session was going to be on Linear Guys Syndicate accompanied by the Old Man who was going to make the most of the bank holiday weekend and join me for a few days. Linear Guys complex consists of 3 lakes that you can fish on the same syndicate ticket, Gaunts, Unity and Yeoman's. Gaunts is a mature lake with fish over 40lb. Unity is the "runs" water of the 3 holding the most fish although the carp do run to mid-thirties and the tench over 10lb.

Last but not least was Yeoman's which is 15 acres and the smallest and has the reputation of being the toughest of the 3 as it has the lowest stock.

We planned to arrive on Saturday afternoon due to Dads work commitments and then fish through to Tuesday; it was a bit optimistic expecting to even get a swim on a busy bank holiday weekend! As we drove through the gates on the gravel track, it takes you along the road bank in between both Unity and Yeoman's. We spotted a swim free on Unity and then almost directly opposite one was free on Yeoman's. We had originally planned to fish together in the same swim and make it bit of a social weekend however the swims were only a short distance apart so we took residence in these. Almost all the swims on Unity were taken so we had little choice.

I chose to stick with my spodding approach that had so well on the Boat Pool and fish over a big bed of bait. The Old Man was also going to spod a chosen area and then fish both rods on pva bags. We had to wait until the following morning for our first run as Dads right hand rod tore off and he was soon into his first Linear fish. It put up a great scrap and soon we could see why; as I did the honours with the net. On the mat lay a beautiful dark chunky tench. It was a magnificent looking fish and the Old Man was anxious as it looked like another PB. I soon put him at ease with a reading of 7lb 12oz it was indeed a PB.

I was going to have to wait a little longer for my first Linear fish, however I learnt a lot about Yeoman's that weekend which stood me in good stead for the coming months. I took a few walks around the lake and spoke to several anglers who had been fishing the venue for a few years, they suggested sticking to Unity as it held more fish however as I returned to my swim, I felt Yeoman's might suit my style of fishing and it seemed less pressured.

Dad added to his tench the following morning with a stunning looking ghostie which weighed over 18lbs, another PB for him as this was his biggest ghost carp. The lake was shrouded in mist as I netted the fish for him and the sun had only risen minutes before.

When fishing for big fish the quality of venue is paramount as far as fish stocks are concerned as you cannot catch what isn't there. Looking back, I believe I picked the right venues for my campaign and my next couple of sessions once again turned up something special.

Mirror Carp – Opportunist Fishing

After his recent success Dad was itching to return to Linear, so I delayed my next session so that we could fish together, we intended to target Unity on this occasion. As the van pulled up the gated entrance, I jumped out and entered the digits on the combination lock, four little numbers that allow you into a world of angling dreams.

We arrived on a Sunday around midday; our thoughts were that most weekend anglers would be packing up for the drive home, leaving us optimum opportunity to pick a fancied swim. On arrival, we did not unload all the gear, instead as usual we carried a couple of buckets of bait each and if a swim was free that we fancied we would leave our buckets in it and return to the van for the remainder of the tackle. On walking around the lake, we found a nice double swim with lots of open water in front of us, to the left was a very interesting looking reed lined bay area, perfect for summer carp. We felt this was the right choice so we dropped our buckets in the swim and returned to the van to load up the barrows.

As I walked back to the van I stuck my head through a gap in the waterside bushes that overlooked a very enticing bay further down the lake towards the carp park. The water on these gravel pits is gin clear and I was amazed at what I saw. Weed rising from the bottom of the lake which stood 3 feet tall, swan mussels and best of all several large carp were cruising around on or near the surface, a couple of them were certainly over 20lb and most were good doubles. It was like looking into an aquarium, I could even make out the individual scales on each fish, I was mesmerised for a few minutes. One of the exciting aspects of angling apart from catching fish is observing them in their natural environment. I crept away from the bay and rushed back to the van as I decided to make the most of this opportunity. I rigged up my 1.75lb barbel rod which I had brought along in the case the chance of floater fishing arose, the reel holding 10lb line to which I attached a light controller float straight through to a size 8 hook to which I super glued a dog biscuit to. Within minutes I was ready to cast out.

As I returned to the bay the carp were still cruising leisurely on the surface and my first cast fell amidst the shoal of fish. The first carp to show interest was one of the smaller ones, so I reeled the bait in as my intention was to land one of the bigger fish. I recast with minimum disturbance and flicked out a few freebies. The sun was now beating down as it dazzled off the surface of the lake, a large carp rose to take one of the biscuits, then she made her way toward my baited hook. I could not believe what I was witnessing, several large carp in one area and one of them was about to show interest in my mixer! It was a mirror and one of the largest in the group; I had no intention of reeling the bait away this time.

A big pair of lips broke the surface and sucked in a dog mixer, it was the hooked offering and as the carp turned away the line went tight, I struck and all hell broke loose as it sped away attempting to find sanctuary in the weed beneath it. As I was only using 10lb line it was inevitable that the carp would reach the weed bed, however I kept the line tight with as much pressure on the fish as the rod would allow. It was a memorable fight; the barbel rod spent most of the next 10 minutes at full curve as I persuaded the fish away from the weed and closer to the bank. At one point the hooked carp was joined by another obviously interested in the commotion and swam behind her for a while before departing leaving me with a stunning memory. Dad was on hand with the landing net as I eased the fish over the rim with a massive sigh of relief. It was a stunner and one that I would remember due to a remarkable feature. Her right eye was completely black and protruded like a marble. I later learned the fish was imaginatively named "Black Eye!"

She was easily my biggest surface caught carp and at 26lb 10oz. After a few photos, I slipped her back into the crystal-clear water and watched her swim away in the now vacant bay. I had been on the fishery less than an hour and I had bagged a big carp, it was opportunist fishing which cannot be ignored, if the chance of catching a big fish comes your way, out of the blue, you have to go for it. It would have been very easy for me to find a swim, set my bivvy up and send out a couple of bottom baits with pva bags and sit back, however, observation is very important in fishing. Always be aware of your surroundings and what is happening on your water, it might lead to an unexpected capture.

We set up in the midday heat; sweat beaded my brow as I hammered in another bivvy peg. Dad heavily baited the reed fringed bay to his left and placed his baited rig amongst the free offerings, not expecting a quick response this was a bait and wait tactic, or so he thought. Both my rods were cast out with pva bags looking to pick up the odd bite, I did not go with my favoured mass baiting approach as I was fishing into open weedy water, I thought single hook baits may give me a better chance. We didn't have to wait long for our first run, it was Dads left hand rod positioned in the bay area that went off and after a decent fight he was soon admiring a lovely tench around the 6lb mark and this was shortly followed by another in the 5lb bracket. Looking back, I only wish I had taken more photographs of those tench as they were stunning, however in the days before the likes of Instagram and social media many anglers rarely took photos of all the fish they caught or edgy shots of the rod set up! Also with Dad landing a good 7lber on his last trip these seemed average fish. During that first day, the Old Man managed about a dozen tench to almost 7lb and I landed a single figure carp. We retired to our bivvies' happy with another day on Linear.

The bay was alive with fish on the second day and from first light the Old Man was catching tench steadily throughout and again ended up with over a dozen tench in the 6lb bracket, he also lost a good fish which was almost definitely a carp which managed to bury itself in the reeds before the hook departed. My fishing on that day was slow, it was very hot and I managed another single figure carp. There were signs of the fish spawning as they chased each other in certain parts of the lake, that's not a good sign to fishermen as it often means that the fishing will be very difficult until the annual event has abated. I even returned to the bay I had success in the day before on the surface, however I watched the water for an hour and no carp materialised. I did notice the wind was not pushing down this end of the lake today so maybe that was a factor. I returned to base camp and recast my rods. We stayed up chatting into dark before retiring to our bivvies', only to be woken at first light by the bite alarm on Dads "tench" rod!

That third day turned out be hotter than the previous two, with blazing sunshine the carp were clearly getting into the swing of spawning. Over several minutes I noticed a few carp showing towards the middle of the lake, a distance of around 100 yards. I decided to try and have a go for them, considering I had only been fishing between 50-60 yards up until now, my rig required a couple of tweaks to reach the showing fish. I reeled the rig in, replaced the pear lead with a long distance 3oz lead, left the pineapple pop up on however this time I did not attach a pva bag which would help me gain valuable yards. I took position at the water's edge and gave the rod an almighty cast out to the showing fish. The lead splashed down in the vicinity, which surprised me a little as I was not normally used to fishing long distances, placed the rod in the rest and switched the bite alarm back on in the hope that an inquisitive carp may fancy my brightly coloured hook bait.

In the meantime, Dad had landed another tench. Over those few days the Old Man amassed about 40 tench, a couple of them were low 7's however most were in the 6lb bracket, it was incredible fishing and a very memorable session for us both. For anyone who enjoys to target tench, Unity is a great water to pursue them on.

After not too long the distance rod had attracted some welcome attention as the bobbin shot up to the rod as the line went taught, it was not a screamer due to the fact I was fishing in weed. The carp did not have to travel far as I also had my bait runners locked up and he struggled to pull line from the spool. As the rod took on its fighting curve I had to pull the fish through the weed bed, it came through steadily and in open water the fish started lunging and made several good runs. It felt like a decent fish, certainly bigger than the singles I had caught the day before.

As the carp neared I could tell it wasn't going to make the 20lb mark, however it was a fit spirited mid double and always welcome especially as the carp were about to embark on their spawning ritual. Once in the net the scales confirmed a good fish and being a scorching day, I decided to get in the water with the fish to cool off while Dad took a few shots.

15/06/2004

It turned out to be another successful session, the carp became difficult to catch, however I had managed a big carp off the surface which resulted in a surface caught PB and Dad had his best tench session ever. Before we left the complex, I decided to take another walk around Yeomans so as to become a bit more familiar with the swims. Although it had a reputation of being the toughest of the 3 due to the lower stocking density, my instincts were telling me to start there on my next visit. Due to the lower stock, it did attract fewer anglers, this also appealed to me. On my walk around the lake I found the swims engaging, they held lots of natural mature features, my mind was made up; I would target Yeomans.

The drive along the M4 became a familiar affair; it was a trip that I now relished, at the end lay 5 days of searching for big fish. Since my last visit to Linear and the capture of "Black Eye", I decided to set myself a Carp Challenge. It would involve catching a 26lb+ carp from each of the 3 syndicate lakes at Linear. I chose not to include my last capture, which meant I would have to target all 3 lakes over the coming months. I believed a challenge would give me a goal to chase and keep me on my toes. As I pulled up in the carp park, it began to spit with rain and an almost gale force wind was blowing, stark contrast to the conditions on my last visit. It was approaching 1pm as I walked the perimeter of the lake to choose y swim.

The wind was punishing the east bank and it looked very uncomfortable. Normally I would recommend fishing into a head wind, however on this occasion the wind felt cold and unpleasant. I opted for the opposite bank, the tall trees offered some protection against the biting wind, also I was going to be here for several days and the wind had been forecast to change direction. The rule on the venue is no vehicles to be driven around the lakes, so I parked as close to the lake as possible off the path, loaded my barrow, returned the car to the car park, then pushed the loaded barrow to my swim. The strong wind didn't help and tilted me off balance a couple of times. As the lake was all new to me each swim I fished I would cast the marker rod out to find any features then write them in my diary, for future reference. A few casts and 10 minutes later I had a good idea what lay in front of me.

There seemed to be a gravel patch about two thirds out between me and the island, beyond this gravel the bed was much softer. There was also a bit of weed between me and the gravel patch, nothing too serious, a bonus actually. Another find was a gravelly area below the nearside shelf, in about 6 feet of water roughly a rod length out, surely the tench would be patrolling along this feature. I would be using 3 rods from now as the water had a low stock of carp and I required the best possible chance of catching fish. First rod was cast as tight as possible to the overhanging trees on the island, which carried a pineapple pop up. Second would be on the gravel patch baited with Assasin8 boilie and a boilie stringer (no spodding just yet I'll explain shortly), and the third rod destined to be fished in the margins on that appealing patch of gravel below the shelf loaded with a Maple8 boilie. On this rod, I put half a dozen spoons of spod mix and a handful of boilies. My choice not to spod the far area was a simple one. Tufted ducks and coots = bait robbers! I noticed on my last visit every time an angler cast out a spod loaded with delicious feed intended for the carp, the tufties and coots would be on it in seconds, quite often they would pick up the hook bait resulting in a false bite. Not something you relish at 3am! I decided that spodding would be carried out during the hours of darkness so as not to attract too many birds.

Considering it was nearing the end of June it was a lot cooler than it should be, during the day I spotted no signs of carp at either end of the lake. It was late evening; I rebaited all 3 rods ready for the night, switching the pop up to a Maple8 boilie, also casting that to the gravel patch joining the other rod. As it drew dark I readied the spod rod, which was already clipped up to the required distance and I proceeded to bait up using half a bucket of spod mix. My clever plan of spodding under the cover of darkness did not deter the bird activity, albeit there were less of them, they still dived down to reach the bait during the night, which resulted in a few bleeps every so often. The wind persisted during the night; thankfully y bivvy was robust and kept me well sheltered during this episode.

I woke at 5am the following morning to bright sunshine accompanied by a light breeze, maybe things were looking up. After several cups of tea, around 8.30am my Assasin8 rod tore off leaving the bite alarm screaming a one toner. There seemed to be weight to the fish as I struck into an angry carp which proceeded to take another 20 yards of line, gradually I slowed the fish as it kited to my left towards the reed lined margin. These mature gravel pits boasting bulrushes, over hanging branches and plentiful weed beds are beautiful places to fish, however its these features that the carp attempt to find sanctuary in when hooked and this one was no different. It was now 40 yards directly to my left along the same bank. I increased the pressure on the fish with side strain as it become dangerously close to the substantial bulrushes. The added pressure paid off as I worked the fish into open water, I dipped the middle rod tip into the lake so as not to cross lines. As the carp now plodded in front of me, I netted a fine mirror at the first attempt. It was a plucky plump carp at 20lb 3oz. The sun dipped behind a cloud as I took a few self takes with my recently purchased digital camera.

Twice during the day tufties stole the boilie of the hair, both times giving what sounded like good runs on the alarms, resulting in me dashing for the rods, only to see a tufted duck surface with a beak full of boilie! Apart from that the day passed uneventful, even on my daily walk around the lake I failed to spot any carp activity. It rained heavily for an hour during the evening; it really was turning into a wet summer. Before midnight I landed a male tench over 5lb on the Maple8, those tench love that flavour. It felt cold and damp as I recast the rod in the dark, feeling the lead down for a positive thump on the gravel. I had a few more bleeps on the alarm during the early hours from ducks – don't those things ever sleep!

The following morning brought glorious sunshine a little cloud and gentle breeze blowing from left to right. For the first time, this week I noticed some carp, a group were cruising over a large gravel bar at the bottom of the island to my right, obviously following the wind. I wound the rods in, took just one and a few essential bits and headed a few swims down which would allow me to cover the area. It wasn't very deep where the carp were due to a gravel bar, a single boilie and pva stringer was cast into the area again feeling for the donk down. As I sat there with the rod positioned on the floor it felt warm in the morning sunshine as I engaged the bait runner. I sat on the unhooking mat, watching and waiting for a couple of hours hoping for a take that never materialised. Slowly over time the carp drifted away one by one.

On returning to my swim I decided to change all 3 rigs. So far, I was using inline leads, which I had total confidence in, however, with the lake holding so much weed I felt a lead clip system would have the advantage of dumping the lead if a big carp found its way into a thick weed bed, hopefully it would help me land any future fish. I felt this would be the best rig going forward.

The night that followed was a frustrating one. Several times carp crashed over my spodded area, without so much as a bleep on the alarms. I prayed my decision to change the lead set up was not to blame for the lack of bites. I had to have confidence in my rigs and not every showing carp result in a hooked fish. It rained heavily again during the night, only stopping before first light as the sun began to shine brightly over the island and at 5am the bobbin dropped to the ground, as a positive drop back bite resulted in a large tench taking the scales to 7lb 11oz, my equal second biggest. A fat, stocky fish sporting a dark back and bright belly.

The sun shone long enough to dry the bivvy out and I was packed away by 1pm. Before I left I managed to speak with one of the bailiffs on the complex, only 2 other fish had come out during the week, one being a 24lber from the road bank. I left satisfied, I accepted the fishing was going to be tricky however that made the catches more rewarding. Another 20 under my belt that was to be my aim on each visit.

My next session was very quiet, resulting in just one male tench over 5lb. I moved swims twice with no success. No carp came out to any angler on Yeomans that week even though the weather was again wet and windy which would be ideal conditions for gravel pit carp. On a positive note, I did manage to prebait a few margin spots in preparation for my next trip.

Early July and the blazing hot sunshine meant it felt like summer for a change. The welcome breeze made it feel pleasantly cooler as I made my ritual stroll around the lake, revealing just two other anglers, they turned out to be mates, here for the week. I spent a few minutes chatting to them, they had not caught or seen any signs of any fish so far. They were fishing the road bank, this meant I had the rest of the lake to myself for now. I, myself did not spot any noticeable carp activity so I decided to fish at the top end of the lake, furthest from the carp park, in a swim I prebaited on my previous session. The wind was blowing towards that end of the lake which was an added bonus. The barrow felt lighter this week; perhaps I was becoming used to the heavy load.

With the weather being so hot, I kept thinking that the carp must be near the surface. I quickly set the bivvy up, stuffed it full with the entire contents of the barrow, and armed with the floater rod, net and mat I zipped up the door and headed for the little bay on Unity lake. As I peered through the bankside greenery, my polarised glasses revealed a host of big carp, including a couple of large ghosties; I observed them for a few minutes before I catapulted in a few mixers. I could watch big carp all day long, they are stunning in their watery world. The fish were reluctant to take the freebies at first. Suddenly a swirl, as a small common engulfed a mixer. I cast in my rig with flavoured cork ball acting as a hook bait. A couple of big carp showed an interest, however it was a frustrating hour, with the carp looking spooky and none of them took the bait that afternoon, again it was a pleasure to witness such an array of fish. As I looked around the Unity, I could see several anglers inside their bivvies' stretched out on their comfortable bedchairs, they don't know what they are missing! I returned to Yeomans's.

During this time, a couple more anglers had arrived, however they also decided to set up close to the carp park, leaving the top half of the lake to myself, just as I preferred, solitude. As I stood in my swim I devised my plan of attack. The margins to my left and right were lined with thick reed beds and cried out to be fished, casting would be little more than an under-arm flick. The third rod was to be fished into open water directly in front of me into a weed bed. The two margin spots had been prebaited the previous week, so I would be hopeful of them producing. Since my last session I went along to my local tackle shop and purchased plan B! A few years prior I fished a small syndicate lake near Gloucester, when the fishing became difficult I used a boilie by Solar called Club Mix, it was an instant hit with the carp and I caught steadily. If you've never used Club Mix I can highly recommend it, especially when combined with the glug, it smells both savoury and fishy, a great fish attractor. The carp seem to love it so that's good enough for me. It was this that was my plan B, I baited as usual, spod mix with a few handfuls of boilies in the respective areas.

Soon after casting, I received several vicious liners on the right-hand rod, then on the middle rod, just as a large carp came crashing out directly over my spodded bait. I sat there expecting a take at any moment. I lit the stove and filled the kettle and made a brew. Again, the bobbin on the right-hand rod shot up and back down, I left it for a few minutes before I reeled in to check the rig. As I stood reeling in I noticed a small common followed by a small mirror carp to my right meandering through the marginal reeds, perhaps these were the culprits, hitting the line as they passed by. I recast, it was now becoming dark as the day faded into night; I retired to my sleeping bag.

I was abruptly awoken just after midnight to the sound of what can only be described as a man walking through the bulrushes, waving his arms back and forth attempting to create as much noise as possible. Clutching my mallet, I peeled back the sleeping bag and bravely withdrew from the bivvy, pointing the head torch towards the water. As I neared the water's edge, I could not see anyone, the sound waned, however, the reeds remained swaying back and forth, I shone the light into the water. I was greeted with dozens of single figure carp swimming frantically in a group, jostling each other, obviously spawning had recommenced after the cooler spell of weather. As I returned to my bivvy I gave a tent peg a tap with the mallet, as if that was the reason I had picked it up in the first place!

I had been asleep for only a few hours before the alarm on my left margin rod gave a few bleeps, I immediately thought tench and after a lot of head shaking and thrashing, I slipped the net under another plump 5lber. It was around 4.30am, the tench had taken the Club Mix, the sky was a beautiful pale orange, not a breath of wind and the sun already felt warm, this was definitely the calm before the storm. Unfortunately, that glorious start to the day did not last long, by midday a strong north easterly was blowing cold accompanied with heavy spells of rain and to top it all off the coots were giving me false bites! If the weather continues in this fashion it will be unlikely that the margin spots would produce more fish.

The rain during the day had forced me to be bivvy bound for most of it. The wind had gathered momentum and it was turning into a full-blown storm. Around 8pm I noticed a carp crash about 60 yards out, I reached for the binoculars hoping the fish would show itself again. It obliged and a big mirror head and shouldered clean out the water. I had a great view of its large head and thick dark back, it was a good 20. It had crashed out over the weed, so I wound my middle rod in, replaced the boilie with a pineapple pop up and cast out to where the carp had showed. With the rod back in the rests I decided to tighten the guy ropes on the bivvy due to the high winds.

As I hammered in the last peg, I heard a bleep, I held the mallet above the peg and listened, another bleep followed by a few more, I dropped the mallet and headed for my rods. The middle bobbin had completely dropped to the ground, I struck immediately. The rod arched over, whatever I had hooked felt heavy, the rod had only been cast out 5 minutes. I reeled in a few yards, the fish was coming slow but steady, then I felt a definite kick, it was definitely a carp. My only option was to keep the pressure on and pump the mass towards me slowly; the fish kicked again and took several yards of line, I kept applying the pressure as the fish neared the bank. The fish stayed deep as it made another bid for freedom, I eventually managed to pump the fish to the surface including the ball of weed that covered the majority of the carp. I couldn't make out its size due to the low light levels. It didn't give me too much trouble, after a few more powerful lunges I finally slipped the net under the fish including the mass of weed it had gathered. I heaved the whole lot onto the bank and peeled back the mesh. My hands were shaking as I tore away the weed to reveal a big beautiful mirror, sporting a star burst of scales near its tail, with its large head and dark back it was almost certainly the fish I had spotted crashing out. The rain held off long enough to take a couple of photos and the scales went over 27lb. I was ecstatic, it was also part one of my carp challenge complete. It was also another case of opportunist fishing, never be afraid to cast to showing fish, it often means they are feeding and willing to take a hook bait.

As I slipped her back the heavens opened delivering torrential rain and a gruelling wind. I received 2 further takes during the night both from male tench one at about 11pm the other at 1am, on each occasion I received an absolute soaking in the driving rain. A lot of carp anglers class these tench as "nuisance fish" when they are targeting a water, especially low stock waters such as Yeoman's. Personally, I enjoy catching these tench whilst carp fishing, it gives me confidence in my rigs, it means my baited spots are being visited and hopefully in turn will attract the carp that I am searching. However, when it involves me being soaked to the skin, I can only take so much! At this rate, I would be running out of dry clothes.

The following couple of days stayed wet and windy, the fishing was slow, however I kept the bait going in and observing the water for signs of carp. Colin, one of the bailiffs on the complex popped by, you can always hear him before you see him as he drives a loud quad bike, his long blonde hair trailing in the wind, always accompanied by his loyal companion, a fit Springer Spaniel, usually riding "shotgun" in the quads front basket. He informed me that no other carp had been caught from Yeomans's this week and there were now several anglers on the lake. I was glad to have taken my opportunity when I did.

The Old Man arrived on the Friday morning for the weekend and judging by the amount of bait buckets that were squeezed onto his barrow, it could only mean one thing, mass baiting. He had decided he was going to pile the bait in early and make the most of his two days by hopefully attracting the carp into his swim and reap the rewards in the final 24 hours. He settled into a swim just down from myself, which offered him plenty of open water, once he found a clear patch with the marker rod, proceeded to spod out the particle mix and boilies. This took some time and I duly assisted with the spodding while he got his bivvy sorted. The stiff breeze continued and we received some heavy thundery showers during the day, unfortunately no fish made an appearance, we chatted into the evening and retired to our respective bivvies' before sunset, hoping for a carpy alarm call.

The Old Man received lots of vicious liners during the night, perhaps it was smaller fish feeding over the spod mix or maybe he was just unlucky not to have a run, either way something had found the bait. A good hearty breakfast of bacon and eggs set us up for the day and around my 3pm my right-hand alarm went into meltdown as the rod hooped over as a carp tore off with the rig. As I struck into the fish it persisted in taking more line and a memorable fight followed. After several minutes, a fit lean common broke the surface and Dad did the honours with the net. You could see the reason why I had such a fight on my hands, the common was shaped like a torpedo, a solid golden carp and at 19lb 2oz it was another decent fish.

The rest of the day remained warm and as the evening drew on the wind died down leaving a pleasant evening, we had a couple of cans of lager before bed. There has always been a social side to our fishing, we always try our best to catch however we also enjoy our time on the bank and our surroundings, it is a good escape from the daily grind and we always seem to have a laugh when fishing. The couple of hours around sunset are probably my favourite, the vivid colours as the sun drops, the bird life quell their song as they prepare for the night and as an angler a feeling of anticipation of being woken from a screaming alarm which can only mean one thing.

The night passed and the following morning the sun shone in between the heavy cloud cover, conditions seemed good and Dad had kept the bait going in all weekend, I wondered whether his hard work would pay off. Customary bacon sarnies for breakfast, few recasts and we sat back for the remainder of our session. We started leisurely packing away around lunchtime and as always, our rods were the last items to be returned to the holdalls.

As the Old Man attempted the impossible task of repacking his bivvy into his seemingly far inadequate sized carry bag, his middle rod took off as the alarm screeched into a one toner. He quickly and gleefully resigned the packing of the bivvy and hit the run, lifting into a good fish. After all the liners and beeps over the weekend thankfully his heavy baiting had paid off and a good carp tore away attempting to seek sanctuary in the thick weed bed. The Old Man played the fish hard steering it away from the weed and closer to the net. I could now make out it was a good mirror and certainly over the magical 20lb barrier and as it neared the surface of the gin clear water, the stunning linear scale pattern became ever more present as I slipped the fish over the cord.

It took the scales over 24lb however size was irrelevant, it truly was a special looking carp and certainly best of the session, it could have been carved from oak with apple slice scales running along it body. After a couple of photos, I was curious to know what bait it had taken, did he stick with boilie or change to tiger nut to blend in with his particle spod mix? I was a little surprised with the Old Man's reply, "a big fat slug!"

"A what......." I replied back.

During the process of packing away his bivvy the Old Man had come across a big fat black slug hugging the underside of the groundsheet, with nothing to lose he reeled in, hair rigged the slug and cast him out onto the baited area. Within 15 minutes his rod had roared off! What a great way to end the session, talk about opportunist fishing, an impressive carp caught on a natural bait, something to think about!

Common Carp – Fully Scaled Warriors

After my recent success I once again graced the banks of Yeoman's within a few days and as always took a recce around the lake fish spotting and to chat to any other anglers that were fishing. Half way around I spoke with an angler who had already been here 48 hours without putting a fish on the bank and on my return to the road bank I bumped into one of the bailiffs on the venue. On speaking with him he said no reported catches apart from mine and the Old mans had come from Yeoman's in the last 2 weeks! I must have been doing something right, luck certainly did seem to be on my side.

I pondered by the car as I drank from a bottle of water, quenching my thirst after my walk. I already had an idea of where I wanted to fish. The only signs of fish were at the very top end of the lake, a handful of carp cruising around below the surface in and out of the reeds beds. Since my time on the lake I had noticed carp frequented this area often however, anglers were not catching as regular as you would expect especially with the numbers of fish in that area. I came to the conclusion for whatever reason the carp were not feeding in this area on a regular basis and must have been moving away to feed then return to bask near the sanctuary of the substantial reed bed.

I gazed across at Unity, I would have to fish this lake soon if I were to complete my Carp Challenge. It was a lot busier with several anglers already fishing, this was normally the case, due to the higher stock of carp present. I turned back to Yeoman's, the swim I had in mind was about a third of the way down the lake from where I spotted the carp, it offered a dense weed bed which ran the middle of the lake, effectively cutting it in half. My plan was to fish tight up to the weed bed picking off any carp that were patrolling along this feature. The image of carp feeding in and out of the weed was all I required to make my mind up and I reversed the car off the road bank ready to unload the gear onto the barrow.

I stood in the swim and contemplated my options, I ruled out the margins and decided my best attack would be to place two rods towards the weed bed for the duration of my stay. Using the marker rod, I quickly found the edge of the weed and started to feed bounteous amounts of boilies along the edge of this. After several sessions on the lake I made the decision not to feed any particles, I felt the better fish would be seeking out the more nutritional boilie baits now that spawning had dwindled following a recent hot spell. This was probably the reason why not many carp were caught, hopefully with this annual event over, the fish would start to get their heads down on the feed.

I came prepared with several kilos of boilie and as I was only fishing around a third of the way across, I fired them out with a catapult, spreading boilies over a large area along the weed bed. The left-hand rod was baited with double club mix and the right, a single.

The afternoon became sweltering which saw me seek the shade of the bivvy and consume lots of water. I enjoyed the rest of the day, watching the water for signs of fish and listening to the cuckoo's unmistakeable call. No need for a sleeping bag tonight, I drifted off still in my shorts with just a thermal cover over me. I expected my best chance of a bite would be during the cooler part of the day from dusk to mid-morning and this proved to be the case.

As I enjoyed my second cuppa of the morning my ever-reliable Fox Micron indicated a carp had taken the double boilie rod, due to me fishing close to weed my bait runner was set very tight so the carp could not bury itself and find sanctuary in the weed bed, this forced the fish to kite left pulling the rod tip around. I lifted into the fish and it instantly took more line as I eased the clutch off and played an angry carp. I waded into the lake up to my knees so as to gain more side strain, I began to gain some line back as the fish turned into open water towards the weed bed, I had to apply pressure and try and turn his head, in these situations it is important to have total confidence in your rigs and tackle. I angled the rod to the left to turn the fish once more and it seemed to work, for the next 6 or 7 minutes it was a memorable fight, when I eventually saw the fish for the first time, it was a large common, my nerves were at breaking point. I really wanted this fish safely in the net, there were a few heart stopping moments with the carp constantly twisting and turning just inches from the cord then on my fourth attempt I scooped the net under the stunning looking common. I gazed at the fish as it lay in the mesh in the warm shallow water which felt refreshing around my ankles. I made my way out of the lake and lifted the fish on to the waiting mat.

My prize was an immaculate common, probably a little down in weight due to spawning, however the needle read 25lb 5oz, a PB common. I was over the moon. I poured more water over the fish in the bright sunshine before I managed a few photos. Large common carp are not as their name suggests, that common! Majority of fish in our fisheries are mirrors so I feel it always a special occasion when you are lucky enough to land such a fish. I waded out once more to release her, part of me didn't want to let it go and as I parted company the majestic fish swam peacefully into the depths.

Over the next couple of days, the weather stayed warm and the early morning feeding spell continued each day which saw me land a rounded plump mirror of 15lb the following morning and on the third day about 4am another twenty in the shape of an old battler of a carp. It went 24lb 6oz and all the fish that session fell to the double boilie hook bait.

Catfish – A Face Only Their Mothers Could Love

The car window was rolled all the way down for a good reason as I made my way along the M4, the sun shone brightly and the breeze racing through the car cooled me as I past the junction for the Linear Complex. The weather men had predicted a very warm humid spell to remain for the rest of the week so I decided to return to the Boat Pool in search of a big bream.

As with any session, on arrival I grasped a bait bucket and took a stroll around the lake. As I neared "Vince's" swim I noticed a row of bivvies occupying the bank. However, the anglers in question were not fishing for the bream or tench of the Boat Pool but for the famous carp that reside in historic Horton Church Pool. This far bank where I had success in the past was now going to see a lot of activity with anglers casting, socialising and using the bank as a thoroughfare to access the fisherman's lodge. Ever since I started fishing I have sought out the more secluded areas of a fishery and today I felt that I should do the same. I headed for the opposite corner of the Boat Pool and settle into a swim named "The Beach" after it's a gradual sloping gravel bank that's lead to the water.

The swim boasted deep margins and overhanging trees with about 11 feet of water directly in front of me. I opted to fish 3 rods as the swim commanded a reasonable amount of water, 2 margin spots to the left and a rod straight ahead in the slightly deeper water. Half a bucket of my usual spod mix went into each margin spot and half a kilo of boilies went on the third rod. Boilies were fished on 2 rods, with maize on the left-hand rod all using the reliable lead clip system. Prior to darkness the sky clouded over and during the night along with a few line bites I experienced a very heavy brief rain shower.

I had been awake a few hours when I received my first action, at 9am the following morning my bobbin danced and cavorted with the left-hand rod; I lifted the rod and reeled in a plump 6oz roach! As I returned the plucky little fish the right-hand rod went, the buzzer indicating a fish had taken a liking to the bait, I started to play what felt like a lively tench, however it was not to be as the hook parted, leaving me reeling in a leaf strewn rig.

I decided to spod a whole bucket of particle mix over the middle rod hoping to pull some fish into the area especially the bream. I swapped over to a helicopter rig to combat the soft leafy bottom and changed baits from boilies to 2 grains of maize tipped with a buoyant rubber piece of sweetcorn giving a snowman effect and a slower fall through the water making the hook bait sit on top of any debris. Within an hour I had bream rolling in the swim and I received indications almost immediately, however none of them materialised into a run, let alone a fish on the bank. It was a frustrating evening which turned into a frustrating night as I had constant liners, probably small fish toying with the bait, which is one of the disadvantages of not using boilies when there are a lot of silver fish present.

At first light I emptied the rest of the particle mix into the swim, presuming most of it would have been eaten by the silver fish and within a couple of hours the day was already feeling muggy and very sticky. I had noticed that a patch of fizzing bubbles was coming up on the edges of the spodded area. Perhaps the fish were too cautious to feed confidently amongst the carpet of feed, letting the smaller fish enter the area, however the bigger fish feeding around the edges where they felt safer. I sat tight for an hour, and then decided id wasted enough time and repositioned the rod directly off a patch of bubbles that had appeared on the out skirts of the spodded area. I placed the rod back on the rests before sitting on my bedchair contemplating placing one of the margin rods on the other side of the feed.

Within a minute another bleep on the alarm sounded out. Then the bobbin rose surely and steadily towards the rod and remained there with the line as tight a bow string. I was up in a shot and struck into what was a clearly a powerful fish as it kited away taking line. I managed to stop the fishes initial run as I gained a little back on the reel only for the fish to take off again like a steam train, obviously not a tench, my thoughts turned to one of the large carp as the culprit. This went on for another 5-6 minutes, I was helpless to stop the powerful methodical runs of the fish, it would run 10 yards, I would gain 8 back! I still hadn't seen the fish and I was reluctant to bully it towards the surface due to my 15lb hook link and a tiny size 10 hook. It was inevitable that I had to put some serious pressure on the fish at some point or I would be here until nightfall!

As I pumped the fish, eventually the rig tubing broke the surface, only a few feet below I was expecting to see a scaly mirror to appear however the fish turned and a big tail slapped the surface as I realised what I was connected to.

It was one of the famous catfish. I took the rest of the fight steady but firm and when I finally got his head to the surface it demonstrated one its fighting qualities as it swam backwards into the depths, what an exciting experience.

Fifteen minutes after first hooking the fish he was safely in the net and it was yet another PB at a shade over 20lb it was my first catfish. I admired the fish on the mat, if you can admire something that looks like it's from another planet. I photographed the fish, something that was a challenge in itself, they are not the easiest fish to hold up for the camera and the slime doesn't make it any easier either.

Although the catfish wasn't caught by design and effectively I was fishing for another species, when you're on a roll such as I was you appreciate every piece of good fortune that comes your way and this is what makes it such a special year for me. I believe you make your own luck and repositioning the rods proved to be the successful decision on this occasion. Reminiscing about the session later that evening, I believe the reason that none of the other fish showed was due to the catfish being in the area for a prolonged amount of time eventually pushing the bream and tench away in fear of being eaten. I fished on without any further bites and felt luck really was on my side to of caught such a fish, I was away early the next morning before the predicted storm came in.

Roach – Ruby Finned Jewels

Roach are one of the most beautiful and delicate fish that swim in our waters. The smaller fish can be good fun to catch and very obliging, however their larger brethren of over a pound and especially 2 pounds can be a challenge and a worthy prize. Most anglers would probably admit that they admire the hardy roach, for most young anglers a small roach is normally their experience in angling, it certainly was when I was a child. A big roach is a wonderful sight, unfortunately not as prolific as they once were and certainly not fished for in the numbers they once were back in the day, when roach anglers would line the river banks throughout the winter in search of a big red fin, however nowadays you're more likely to see the banks lined with barbel, pike or even carp anglers. The fact that less people fish for big roach today, makes this elusive fish even more special.

It was late summer, I had a couple of days spare before I returned to Oxford for another go at Linear carp, so I decided to go back to where my specimen fishing began, on the banks of River Monnow. The Monnow, a tributary of the Wye, has a long tradition of big roach and chub with specimen size fish falling to anglers regularly in the past however, although you can still catch the big chub, the roach numbers have declined and the bigger roach are becoming increasingly harder to locate.

Being a rather wet summer meant the river had received plenty of rain over the previous months and on my arrival the river flowed above summer level with a nice tinge of colour, not too dark, just fining down after a summer flood. This was the advantage of not having the commitment of a job, being able to hand pick my days to suit the fish I was targeting, I am positive the conditions had a big part in the outcome of the session.

Luncheon meat has certainly been the downfall of the majority of my large chub captures, however whenever possible I will always choose bread flake hook bait, especially when there is the possibility of a big roach and even more so when I am fishing a steady glide as I chose today, a favourite haunt for both roach and chub. My tactics for this session were going to be a bait and wait approach using an open-end feeder filled with mashed bread and bread flake on the hook, instead of opting for my more favoured approach of fishing several swims during the day when pursuing chub. The swim in question has a shallow section upriver which drops into about 6-7 feet of water which flows steadily until the river bed rises again giving about 3-4 feet of water further down the section; all this takes place in about 40 yards of river, giving a lovely steady deeper glide which I intended to place my hook bait.

An old river bailiff once said to me on a day when I was struggling for bites, "if you want to find the fish, find shallow water that flows into deeper water" this is a tip that has stood me in good stead since my childhood days and one that has seen the downfall of many fish, especially chub. If you think about it, it makes sense, the shallow water delivers the food down the drop off similar to a conveyor belt, straight to the fish, which are enjoying the sanctuary of the deeper water. Maximum food for minimum effort.

No walking the entire section fishing various swims today, I was going to be stationary, although I still travelled light, I had the addition of a comfortable chair for my session. On arrival in my swim, I mashed up two loaves of bread in a plastic bucket and fed in a couple of handfuls up stream so it would settle in the deeper water. It was a consistency that it would only just hold in the small feeder I was using until it emptied its contents along the river bed drawing the fish upstream to my baited hook. I scaled down my hook to a size ten on which I impaled a pinch of bread flake about the size of a 10p piece coupled with a soft quiver tip its ideal for roach.

Late summer early autumn is a great time to pursue roach; the river ideally carries a bit of colour which gives the roach confidence to feed during the daylight hours and the fish are actively feeding in preparation for the colder months which lay ahead.

I started the session casting every 5 minutes to build up the swim with mashed bread and hopefully pull some fish into the swim, this seemed to be working within the first half hour I had a few plucks on the quiver tip then the white tip trembled before reaching downward toward the river. My Avon rod came into play as a powerful fish angrily surged for the far bank, it was certainly one of my intended targets and certainly a chub and by the way it pulled not a bad one. The chub in this section average 2lb, this fish felt above average and after a few minutes a pair of white rubbery lips broke the surface as the ripples floated downstream. Before I slipped the net under the chub it attempted one more escape by heading into the near side branches however as I held the rod at arm's length, I steered the fish away from the wooden sanctuary and over the rim of the net. The brassy flanks shone gold in the late summer sun; the mouth looked even bigger as the fish stared at me sporting a fat belly which made the scales pull around to show 4lb, a good start to the session.

During the next few hours I managed a couple of small chub, then mid-afternoon I received a couple of gentle plucks on the quiver tip, I concentrated on the white quiver against the dark shrubs on the far bank, it dipped a couple of inches, I struck and was greeted with a series of head shakes. My presumption was another chublet, however in the back of my mind I was hoping for an elusive Monnow Roach. The fish twisted and turned in the current and soon a flash of silver was visible inches below the surface. It looked too deep to be a dace and lacked the airborne acrobatics of a trout, my pulse started racing at the thought of a decent roach. The Avon rod soon subdued the fish and my cherished prize slipped over the rim of the net against the flow of the river, it was a typical roach, with its silver scales and bright red fins.

After losing a couple of big roach in the past it was a relief to see one in my landing net as I carried it up the bank before unhooking and photographing the fish. I do not fish for roach enough during the river season so when the opportunity comes along you have to make the most of the situation; I edged my bets today and favoured bread flake over luncheon meat. The roach weighed 1lb 8oz, it was another PB, I was certainly on a roll. I admired the fish briefly before slipping her back into her watery home, free to return to her shoal in the steady glide.

I am certain I still would have caught chub if had used luncheon meat as a hook bait however my opportunity of landing a roach would of virtually nil. A lot of angler's lack confidence in using bread flake on the hook, believing that it falls off the hook too easy or the smaller fish rip it to pieces before the bigger fish have chance of taking the bait. It is important to use the freshest bread for the hook as you fold the flake and pinch it on the hook it has to be pliable, if it has dried out it will easily come away in the flow leaving you fishing with a bare hook. As for bread mash, I prefer to leave a couple of loaves exposed to the air for a couple days prior to fishing so that they dry out and when water is added to them in a bucket they make a less stodgy mash, you want to attract the fish into your swim, searching for your hook bait and not over feed them.

*Unfortunately, having moved house a couple of times and the photographs from this session, which were printed off, have become lost. I have searched high and low, checked every disc and SD card I own; however, I cannot locate them. **I have used photos from another session I had later that year**, which leaves me just a tiny bit gutted to say the least!*

Pike – A Royal Appointment

Currently home to the 11th Duke of Marlborough and famously the birth place of Sir Winston Churchill, set 2000 acres of parkland designed by Capability Brown which includes the Great Lake, Blenheim Palace attracts visitors from all around the world, including anglers every year. Previous holder of the British record Tench and home to specimen sized Bream, Roach and Perch, the Pike are the reason why we make our annual pilgrimage to this wonderful historic venue.

Blenheim Palace will always hold a special place in my angling heart not just for the prime fishing but also for the time spent enjoying the Old Man's company over a few beers after a day afloat on the water. Due to the distance we have to travel to the venue we always make a few days of it, book into a B&B and have at least a couple of days fishing. This we have done for many years and will continue to do so in the future.

Fishing is by boat only and these are kept in an old-fashioned boat house a short walk from the carp park. You are issued with a key code for each day and a gentleman named Mick will normally greet you in the morning to make sure everything runs smoothly. After several years of fishing at Blenheim, Mick has been consistent in his advice on where to fish! "Around the bridge" or "in front of the boathouse", is his usual reply.

These two areas are where most anglers head for and normally throw up a fish or two. However, it is best to stay mobile and in doing this you have greater chance of finding the fish.

After a hearty breakfast at the B&B we headed for the car park in the van and as usual there were already a couple of vehicles parked up when we arrived, with a quick scan of the lake I noticed a boat anchored in front of the bridge. The short walk downhill to the boat house is a pleasant one as you pass the gardens including the impressive fountains and you can normally spot the odd pheasant. The wildlife within the 2000-acre estate is abundant and if you are lucky enough you can observe deer and a variety of birdlife including the famous Red Kite.

We organised the boat and I pushed us off using the oar as we slowly drifted out into the stunning lake. It was overcast with a slight breeze and not too cold, conditions looked good as long as they stayed this way. We rowed left from the boat house making our way to the south end of the lake, which is the deepest, being 18-20 feet and becomes narrow. We have found the piking to be less prolific in this area however, when you do hook a pike they tend to be bigger than average, so it always worth spending some time here. As usual we would stop every 50 yards or so and put the anchors down and fish for at least half an hour in each spot until we reached the top of the lake.

Using lures has transformed our pike fishing, not just on Blenheim also on other venues as well. Our catch rate increased considerably, however we still use one deadbait rod each in case the pike are not willing to chase lures and are looking for an easy meal. Anchoring no more than 20 yards from the bank we use the overhanging trees and bankside vegetation as features to fish to. Pike use these to ambush unsuspecting prey fish so quite often the open featureless areas of the lake so not produce any fish. Luckily, we did not have to wait long for our first fish and in our second swim of the day I landed a single figure pike on a rubber shad. These rubber shads have caught us countless predators on stillwaters and rivers over the years and remain one of our favourite type of lures to this day.

The deep water did not produce, so we made our way north towards the Grand Bridge, again stopping every so often and casting along the tree line. After a couple of hours fishing we had managed a brace of pike each up to 12lb, both falling to lure tactics.

The water around the bridge is the shallowest on the venue, around 3 feet, the majority of our fish caught here have been smaller and today was no exception as a couple of greedy jacks soon succumbed to our lures. It was turning into an enjoyable session and any signs of my hangover were all but forgotten! 6 pike by lunchtime all on the lures. About 200-250 yards from the Grand Bridge is an area with a depth around 10 feet which has some weed growth and is between the shallower water around the bridge and a deeper area towards to the far bank, generally a consistent area for pike so we decided to move here next.

We stopped here for a bit longer so we could eat our lunch and have a deserved cup of tea. As we took a short break from casting the lures around, Dads deadbait float bobbed then sailed away, not wasting anytime he lifted the rod causing the braid mainline to rip off the surface of the lake before he struck into his third pike of the day. It was a spirited fight with the fish almost tail walking as it neared the boat before I slipped the circular net under the fish, a low double as he posed for photos before being returned.

Conditions remained favourable with overcast conditions and a slight ripple on the water, hopefully there would be more to come as we got into the afternoon and thoughts of returning towards the boat house, again along the tree lined bank. However, after the Old Man's success we resumed lure fishing in this area and I was rewarded with another low double. This time a slightly pug-nosed pike, this is when the lower jaw protrudes the upper jaw, this does look odd however it clearly does not affect the pikes hunting or eating abilities with this fish being in good condition.

After a couple more swims had been fished we had now banked 8 pike between us all but one falling to lure tactics. It was an hour before dusk as we settled into our last swim of the day. It was to the right of the boat house in about 10 feet of water, there were remains of a reed bed against the bank with a very attractive overhanging tree. Deadbaits were cast towards the bank and we engaged the lure rods for the last time that day. As is often the case it is not unusual to hook into a pike within the first few casts and Dads lure was taken as he slowly retrieved it away from the overhanging branches of the inviting tree. I put my rod down to help land his fourth fish of the day, another typical Blenheim pike which are normally quite stocky fish and at around 9lb gave a good scrap with Dad feeling every shake of the head through his braid mainline. Quickly unhooked and slipped back to fight another day.

The use of braid main line for lure fishing is a must in my opinion as the advantages over mono are numerous. The main advantage is the feel and vibration through the line helps the angler get an understanding of exactly what is happening under the water. You can tell the difference between weed, rocks and when a fish takes a bite at the lure. My next cast was no different to any other I had done that day, apart from the take! When I cast out especially with rubber shads I keep the lure on a tight line and feel for it to touch the bottom, as it does this the rod tip springs back as the line falls slightly limp. As I felt the lure fall through the water, it did not have chance to reach its destination and my rod tip pulled towards the lure, it had been taken on the drop. I struck the rod setting the hook as my sixth fish of the day took line as she bolted off. Immediately it went on a powerful run forcing the spool to spin as she took more line, I slowed the fish as Dad reeled in the deadbait rods to avoid tangles, this felt as though it would be the biggest of the day. I remember the fight vividly, throughout I was certain the hook would pull as you so often do when you realise you are attached to a better than average fish.

The pike kept making strong runs, luckily most of them into open water, this went on for several minutes, I was using a medium lure rod which absorbed the pike's lunges and head shakes. My first glimpse was as it neared the boat and a big tail swirled at the surface as it headed towards the depths. By now I knew it would almost certainly be a PB and I made sure I had every chance of landing it the fish, I insisted the Old Man pull up the anchor ropes. In the past I had lost a very big pike from Blenheim around the anchor ropes I did not want a repeat. As he hauled the anchors up in double quick time, we immediately started drifting towards the bank and the snags! Maybe not such a good idea now I would have to contend with them.

On the surface the fish powered back and forth along the boat still out of range of the net. She was tiring and with one last effort with the lure rod using all its power, I managed to get her head up and the Old Man slipped the net under an athletic pike. I kept the pike in the water as he rowed away from the overhanging trees and we lowered the anchors once again to hold position. The pike had engulfed the six-inch shad which we quickly removed with the long nose pliers. On the unhooking mat she looked big although not a twenty, it was going to be another PB in my incredible year. The scales proved this at 17lb 10oz it was my biggest indeed.

She was an impressive beast and shortly after releasing her we were in the bar celebrating with a few beers. I would advise all pike anglers to visit Blenheim at some point in their lives, a venue steeped in history, I feel it is the equivalent to a carp fishers Redmire. Over the years most of our pike have fallen to lure tactics however the biggest pike fell to the Old Man on a smelt deadbait, which weighed over 28lbs, that is why we always take the deadbait rods, you just never know.

We fished the following day, day however without so much as a touch on the lures by midday we decided to visit the boat yard I had recently contacted as we were half way there anyway and within a matter of hours I was the proud owner of a boat!

Zander – All Aboard

The thought of owning a boat on the River Severn had been a vision of mine from the moment I watched the fishing series "Predators" on television. One particular episode featured Matt Hayes (who I later went on to meet whilst fishing the Severn) where he took his boat onto the Severn and targeted the Zander of this mighty river. It was truly inspiring and as an avid lure angler it looked to be a real adventure being able to fish swims that were not accessible from the bank. So, after a couple of months of looking through the pages of Boat Mart, on the last day of our recent Blenheim Palace trip, that resulted in my pike PB, we decided to pack up a little earlier and head over to a boat yard after a quick phone call to the owner.

On arrival he had just 2 boats in my price range, one of which I took an instant liking; it was a perfect fishing vessel. The Orkney Strikeliner with cuddy, 16 feet in length powered by a 25hp Mariner outboard, it looked truly impressive. After a quick tour of the boat and instructions on the gadgets and engine we negotiated a few extras including free delivery to Upton Marina where the boat was to be moored. Although the boat was on the heavy side it didn't matter as I planned to keep it moored up in the one place and did not intend to tow it to various venues. Delivery was to be just a week later.

As the 4x4 pulled into the carp park the boat looked striking with its brand new red cover and new coating of anti-foul. I decided to keep the boat on the trailer for the first couple of days to give me a chance to touch up a couple of areas with gel coat to protect it. Myself and the Old Man didn't want to delay the launch too long as there was only a month left of the river season. Within a couple of days, the boat was launched and as it floated upon the Severn water for the first time I named her "Predator". I spent the next hour familiarising myself with the manoeuvres, lowering the anchor and reading the echo sounder, making the most of the calm water of the marina before we took to the main river and had to deal with the flow of Britain's longest river.

We returned within a couple of days armed with the piking gear including our 10' 6" dead bait rods. The shorter length of the rods makes them far more manageable in the confines of a boat, especially with two anglers, although the Strikeliner boasted plenty of room and is very comfortable vessel to fish from. That first weekend afloat was a real eye opener for both of us.

Being organised is probably the biggest single aspect of boat fishing, making sure all the essential items are to hand, with all excess items stored away so the deck is clear and you're less likely to trip over. We were soon familiar with lowering and raising the anchor and judging the distances required when reversing into a swim. As with most predator fishing, being mobile normally proves to be the best tactic, especially on a large river such as the Severn. So, we spent 45 minutes in each swim and after a good 8-hour session, that's a lot of raising and lowering a 10kg anchor plus the chain, we were tired and fishless.

Our biggest lesson learnt that first weekend was our bait selection. We had never fished the Severn before let alone caught a Zander or Pike from the depths of this magnificent river. Having fished the Wye for Pike for many years, using sea dead baits wasn't a problem, the Wye pike would be enthusiastic seeing a herring or an oily half mackerel sitting on the bottom. The Severn predators were not so enthusiastic as we were about to find out, so as that first weekend afloat progressed, without so much as a pull on the float or a twitch on the rod, we went home fishless and scratching our heads. The swims we fished must have held predators; we fished dozens of swims that weekend, over hanging trees, wooden structures, inlets, outlets including some very deep water. A little research was required before I returned to target those elusive fish.

With quick scan of the internet it seemed that these Severn pike preferred moving baits in the form of lives or sink and draw, forget big sea dead baits static on the bottom. It also became obvious that Zander prefer fresh coarse dead's or even better a spirited live bait. I had been lure fishing for predators far more and it had increased my catch rate on many venues, as proved by the downfall of many Blenheim Pike, so on my next visit to the boat I was accompanied by my vast array of lures, nothing moves more enticingly through the water than a well worked lure. We decided to start fishing within the marina on our next visit as the river level was slightly higher than our previous trip and this proved to be a good tactic.

As we worked our lures close to the other moored boats and the wooden pontoons, it didn't take long before the Old Man took first blood, not a huge fish but it was a start and a massive confidence boost.

Our lures seemed to do the trick in the confines of the marina, it proved a hotspot on many occasion especially when the river was carrying extra water, the fish would congregate in the calm waters instead of having to battle the strong current of the main river. However, when the river levels were low it was the opposite and the main river was the place to be. That day we went on to catch a few pike all around the 5-6lb bracket, we even caught a pike from the main river later that day, however those Zander were still eluding us.

With just a few weeks before the river season I was determined to catch my first Zander, so I tried a new tactic – live baits. Within a couple of days, I was back on the boat, the water looked perfect with a slight tinge of colour and back at winter level. The floating pontoon was illuminated with dim lights as I made my way to the boat, it was still dark and the sun had yet to rise. I was hoping the zander would feed in the half light, just as the sun slowly crept up I made my first cast, this time I came armed with only my lure fishing kit, the rubber lure splashed down and I made my first retrieve stood in the back of the boat.

Within a few casts I was into my first fish, was this to be my first Zed? it fought differently to the pike we had caught, then I caught a glimpse of the culprit, a fine-looking perch. All predators take advantage of these low light conditions so it was no surprise that a perch had taking a liking to the 6" rubber shad.

A couple of jacks soon followed before I decided to make my way onto the main river. It was a quiet day; I moved swims several times, although I could only tempt one more pike around 5lb. The main tactic is to fish along the over grown banks of the river and slowly make your way down a stretch fishing every 60 yards or so, trying to cover as much water as possible, also the zander enjoy the cover of the overhanging branches that line the river.

As it turned out I had to wait until my next session to land my first zander and with a just a couple of weeks of the season left, again I found myself fishing at first light with my reliable rubber shad which was snaffled by a perfect looking zander, I was well chuffed, another first, only around 4lb however that didn't matter, I went out to catch a zander and I did, the fact it was on a lure made it even more special.

Before the season was out, I went on to catch a few more Schoolie zander including several on float fished live Rudd. On the last day of the season I managed a superb live bait caught 15lb + pike which was also a river pb for me at the time. The vivid colouration made it stunning and a special looking fish.

Over the years we went on to catch dozens of zander from various stretches all falling to either lures or live baiting tactics. The rubber shads were invaluable and seemed to work very effectively on the Severn. I always use braid for my predator fishing whether it lures, dead or live baits which I think is very important especially when it comes to using lures. The zander seemed to feed differently to the pike, sometimes when reeling in you would receive plucks and pulls where a fish is biting the lure, on one occasion as soon as I felt one of these plucks, I immediately stopped reeling and let the lure fall to the bottom of the river. To my amazement the rod tip pulled around, I struck was into a fish which turned out to be a zander, this never happened with pike. It seems that the zander will chase a bait, take a bite at it, attempting to wound it in some way, then casually swim up to the bait to engulf it. That tactic proved the downfall of many zander and although I never got amongst the big specimens the Severn is famous for, we rarely blanked after those early sessions. The Old Man went on to catch a fine zander over 7lb on a trotted live bait along with about 10 other zander and a few pike from a slack on the main river, which turned out to be a real red-letter day.

Another red-letter day I recall was a mild overcast day in October, when the perch went on a fry feeding frenzy and during a manic few hours I landed around 30 perch half of them going over 2lb, all close to the entrance of the marina, there must have been hundreds of perch corralling silver fish working as a team and reaping the rewards.

Below are a few photos of some of the fish we had the pleasure of catching during our time on the mighty Severn.

Carp Challenge - Conclusion

We were now well into the month of August and if I were to complete my personal carp challenge then I would have to start targeting the 2 other lakes on my ticket, Unity and Gaunts. I arrived having already made my decision to fish Unity as I had been away from the venue for at least a couple of weeks fishing on the River Wye for barbel so ideally, I wanted to be within a chance of landing a few carp and with Unity's high stocking I thought it would be the obvious choice.

No walk around the lake required today, I noticed an angler was half way through packing down and preparing to leave, he had been fishing in a particular swim I had fancied fishing in the past, however it always seemed to be occupied. I was not going to let this opportunity pass by. The main reason this swim saw a constant stream of anglers was due to one main feature this swim offered. Around 50 yards to the left was a bay area closed off to fishing from the opposite bank and that was only accessible by casting from this swim. When the wind blew into the bay, often groups of carp would congregate in the relative safety of this area. You could peer through the foliage when stood on its bank and watch the carp feed surrounded by reeds and the inlet pipe. My plan of attack would again be boilie only and lots of them, then fish a bait in the narrow entrance to the bay, any carp entering would have to pass by my freebie and hook bait. I chose to fish only one rod in this area so as not to spook the fish and also back lead for extra precaution.

Baiting up would be easy, when the rods were wound in, I would walk around the bank to the bay and throw boilies in by hand through the branches of the trees, this would give me a very accurate baiting strategy with minimum disturbance. The cast was also fairly straight forward, a 50-yard chuck into the narrow entrance. There was only one snag, literally!

Apparently, there were remains of some old fence posts which were not visible as they were below the water line, it would have to be a hook and hold situation. I tightened the baitrunner in anticipation although they were exciting I could not afford the fish to take off on any screaming runs. Bait was again club mix which had served me well. I baited up with half a kilo by hand and noticed a couple of carp were already frequenting the bay, albeit only low doubles, the fish were present.

My second was cast slightly to my right down the margin shelf solely for tench, I baited this with a handful of boilies and several spoons of particle mix.

As I have mentioned previously in this book, I am quite happy to fish with less rods in a hot spot rather than 2 or 3 and possibly reduce my chances. I believed that the less disturbance of just one lead entering the water would increase my catch rate. Back leading is a good tactic when fishing in corners or entrances to bays as it pins the line down out of sight and the carp can come and go as they please without picking up your mainline, this results in less carp being spooked which gives you a greater opportunity that they will hang around, feed and hopefully pick up your hook bait.

It was a typical August day, near cloudless sky, bright sunshine and a gentle breeze pushing directly into the bay area, perfect I thought. Not long after the bivvy was erected my left-hand rod positioned in the bay, signalled a fish, the rod tip pulled towards the backlead as the alarm rung out. I was soon entered into a tussle with plucky mirror around 9lb, I kept steady pressure on him all the way to the net and he was soon released unharmed. This was going to be an occupational hazard in this swim, it held carp of all sizes, I might have to accommodate the smaller fish until the bigger ones arrive. This was not a problem it was a good confidence boost to catch so early into my session and when the smaller carp feed it normally arouses the attention of the bigger carp who do not want to miss out on a free meal.

The following 24 hours saw me land several carp, a couple more singles and handful of low doubles. I was enjoying the session, I had even landed a tench around 5lb in the morning on the tench rod. With regards to tench, if I only 1 tip to pass on it would be to never ignore the marginal shelf. Despite the size of the pit of lake, you find the bottom of the shelf you will find the tench. Their fondness to patrol this area of the lake is their downfall and is by far the most consistent feature to fish when is search of this alluring species.

During the day the wind had dropped off and with it the bites did to. During the afternoon I managed a mirror that was shaped like a dinner plate and lost another fish to the suspected sunken fence posts. It grew into a pleasant warm summers evening and again I fell asleep under the thermal cover as it got dark.

I was woken at first light by the bite alarm and I speedily threw back the cover and raced to the rod, it hooped over as I applied pressure on the fish, steering it away from the snag which it duly headed for. It felt heavier than the other fish I had landed this session and once again the fish tested my tackle to the limits as it persisted in entering the bay, it did not succeed, my Greys X-Flite persuaded the fish into open water and relative safety. I caught sight of the fish and noticed a bulbous black eye, could it be my old friend from earlier in the season? My first surface caught twenty! Only when it was safely on the mat did I realise it in fact a repeat capture of old "Black Eye", it also looked as if she had gained weight during the summer.

She looked fat and healthy and appeared to of been gorging on angler's boilies over the past few months and as I hoisted her off the ground the needle showed over 28lb it was a personal best and the second part of my challenge completed. The dawn chorus was in full swing as I took a couple of self takes, the sun was rising and it was looking to be another scorcher of a day. It was one of my most memorable sessions, glorious weather, plenty of carp and a PB. I felt by fishing just one rod in that area accompanied with regular introduction of bait over the duration of my session it gave the carp the confidence to feed and keep returning to the area each day.

To complete my challenge, I would next have to target Gaunts, probably the toughest of the lakes on the syndicate due to the competent anglers who regularly fish it and the nature of the lake. With bays, islands and overhanging trees in abundance it was packed with features which made swim choice a bit more difficult. Little did I know it would not be until the new year that I would make my first casts into its waters.

It was early April and the close season had already been in effect on the rivers for the last couple of weeks, the trees were starting to spring into life with new buds and hints of foliage. Spring is my favourite time of the year as nature awakens from the short days of winter and slowly develops new life, as the seasons early flowers flourish and the birds prepare for their eggs to hatch. It is also my favourite time to be out carp fishing, as the sun's rays warm the water, the carp head for the margins and shallows in search of food.

I was heading for Gaunts, I only had weeks left on my ticket and I wanted to desperately complete the challenge I had set myself last year. I did have one other session in March on Gaunts, a last minute 24-hour session which resulted in a blank, however it gave me a chance to walk around the venue and choose a likely area the carp may be when the weather warmed up. I was here for 2 days so swim selection would be important, on arrival I took my usual walk around the lake and saw no visible signs of fish. Being a Tuesday, it was fairly quiet however due to the quality of fish that swim within its waters it always attracted anglers, even midweek.

I decided to fish the first swim you come to on the right-hand bank, immediately to your left in this swim was a carpy looking corner with overhanging trees and a reed lined bank, another bonus was that it could only be reached from this one swim so I wouldn't have to compete with any other angler's baits in the vicinity. I chose to fish just one rod in this corner as I wanted to reduce the amount of lines that were going through the water. I had a large amount of open water in front of me and chose to fish a single pop up, casting to various areas to hopefully pick up a passing fish. The other rod fished in corner would be a boilie only approach, fishing with a single club mix on the hook, I would put about 30 boilies around this get the carp searching for food.

I unloaded the gear and drove the car to the car park. On walking back to my swim, I noticed Ian Poole, full time angler and angling journalist, was fishing the opposite bank on Unity lake, we acknowledged each other so I walked over to see how he was getting on. You often bump into angling journalists at the Linear Complex and as long as you do not out stay your welcome, the ones I have spoken to in the past have always been polite, happy to have a chat about fishing and give advice if required, Ian was no exception. He said he had landed a few carp that day and was fishing a method he has become famous for, solid PVA bags. He was just about to reel in, so I asked if I could watch him tie up his next bag. I have to admit, it is an art form which he makes look so easy, the bags are packed tightly, corners folded in, they are so aerodynamic they sail through the air off the cast.

I wished him tight lines and made my way to my swim on Gaunts, I had a challenge to complete! The rods were the first to be sorted and were soon fishing as I baited up the corner with the catapult. My main tip on any venue big or small is to watch the water as much as possible, especially this time of year as the fish become increasingly become more active. Today was no exception, however I only saw one carp jump which was off the island to my right, which an angler was already covering. The afternoon past and every so often I recast the pop up rod hoping to put it in front of a fish.

Before it got dark I put the stove on for some bacon sarnies and a cup of tea and fired a few more boilies into the corner. I stayed up as long as possible however it had been a long day and I was asleep a couple of hours after it was dark. The night passed without my alarms waking me and I was up at first light, it felt cold and there was a heavy dew on the surrounding grass. A rabbit hopped back into the hedgerow as the kettle warmed on the stove for a much needed early morning cuppa. A few more boilies went into the corner although I had not caught a fish, as well as the carp there are also tench and bream so I'm sure they would have eaten some of the bait. I always feel a little and often approach early in the season is best, a bit like a matchmans tactics, at least you know there is bait in the vicinity and as long as you do not pile it in, it's a tactic that normally produces. I recast the pop up rod to a different area and made some breakfast.

By lunchtime I was wondering whether I had chosen the right swim with the lack of fish activity in the area. I scanned the swim again, the overhanging trees and emerging reed bed looked ideal for early season carp to visit. As I hadn't spotted any other areas with showing fish I decided it was best to have faith in my original choice. Early afternoon my faith was restored as I spotted a carp head and shoulder in the corner in the area where my freebies were. I fired a handful of boilies out once more knowing fish were in the area and sat back. Most of the anglers had to pass my swim as they returned to their cars to replenish their stocks or visit the toilet block so I had a pretty good idea of what was happening on the lake. Only one fish had been out in the last couple of days and that was to an angler fishing the margins at the opposite end of the lake.

Gaunts is a very pretty lake packed with features and if you enjoy targeting carp in the margins, such as myself then you will love fishing on this venue. It had been dark for about an hour when the alarm on my corner rod gave a bleep, followed by more bleeps, not a screamer but something was hooked and I quickly lifted into what was obviously a substantial weight. Immediately the fish felt heavy however it was not a classic fight, the fish was dogged using her weight to go on slow deliberate runs and with a bit of patience I soon had her into open water. Being early in the season with the water being cooler, perhaps this had an effect on the way the carp fought. It was still a long way out and it was near the surface as I noticed a swirl in the dark. I took my time, no need to rush this one, there were no heavy weed beds so it was just a case of gaining line and easing her toward the bank.

Minutes later she was in the range of the net, with the head torch on I guided her over the cord. She looked impressive in the mesh and in the torch light I recognised her as "Two Tone" I believe she last came out the previous December. Her fins were massive and she could have been any weight, she looked heavy, certainly more than 26lb and I was confident I had completed my challenge. Scales zeroed, I hoisted her in the weigh sling, 27lb 8oz. I had done it. After a couple of self takes in the dark I admired her once more and returned her to the margins where she swam away strongly. I was happy and felt privileged to of caught such a stunning fish and was over the moon at achieving my challenge I had set and with so little time left to do it.

As it transpired that was to be my last visit to the famous Linear Syndicate complex. After having taken a year off it was almost time to look for a job. My time on Linear will forever be a memorable one, I learnt new tactics, met dozens of talented anglers and was lucky enough to of caught some very memorable special fish.

I have always thought about re-joining the syndicate, however the old saying is "You should never go back, things will never be the same" and in this case, they probably will never be, well not for me. Likened to a holiday romance, we danced, laughed, kissed and shared secrets, before going our separate ways, some things are best left as you remember them.

Pop Ups – Why Do They Work

As you would have gathered from reading "Fishing the Dream" pop ups have featured several times when in pursuit of carp. Quite often they have resulted in a fish which has been the only capture of that session. For a single bait to out fish another which is surrounded by tempting freebies is remarkable however it does happen quite often. I believe there are several factors involved when deciding to fish a pop up for carp which I will go into in more detail.

Firstly, it is important to tie the rig correctly, below is a picture of the rig that has caught me dozens of carp over the years, it is a straight forward pop up rig, I believe in keeping things simple. Some anglers prefer to use split shot on their hook link to counter balance the bait, however I prefer to use putty or the new sinkers that attach to the line. My reason for persisting with putty is that it is malleable and soft, it simply peels off if the carp get amongst weed or debris, where as a split shot may damage and weaken the hook link if it pulls against it.

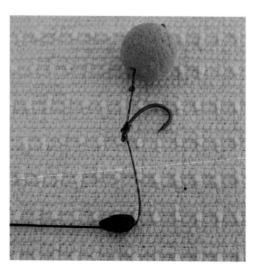

If you are fishing over a soft bottom such as mud or silt then a popped-up bait may be your only option so as not to bury your hook bait and reduce your chances of catching your prize carp. Carp will feed in silted areas and that is why it's important to present a bait there correctly and one that is wafting around under their nose will greatly increase your chances. I will rarely use a pop up over a hard gravel lake bed; normally opting for a wafter or bottom bait in that situation.

Majority of situations will see me using a brightly coloured pop up, with my favourites being washed out pink or yellow, normally in a fruit or sweet flavour. For this reason, I rarely use hemp or pellets as feed when fishing a popped-up bait as this will result in the carp being preoccupied feeding on it's nose in the mud and often ignoring my hook bait. I am looking for the carp to up end every so often, so for this reason I will normally fish a small scattering of boilies around the hook bait to keep the fish interested and searching for another boilie.

Sometimes when waters are pressured with many anglers and dozens of kilos of bait being thrown in, the carp can become wary of big beds of bait. I can recall such a session a few years ago where bait boats are permitted on the venue. It turned out the most successful anglers on there were using single baits or pop ups, it seemed the carp avoided these big beds of baits deposited by the anglers using the bait boats, becoming suspicious of them, probably having been caught whilst getting their heads down in the past. The effectiveness of the single bait is that curiosity gets the better of the carp and they will investigate a brightly coloured boilie where as they will sometimes avoid mass baiting.

My preference for lead systems is to fish a pop up with a lead clip or helicopter set up. I feel these give the best presentation especially when fishing in lakes with a softer lake bed.

Casting to showing fish is also highly recommended. This proved successful when I landed a large mirror that equalled my personal best at the time. If a brightly coloured pop up is cast directly to a showing carp then it has a good chance of being taken, normally carp that head and shoulder are feeding and when you cast a bright bait in that area it has the advantage of standing out when the fish is actively searching for food. It is amazing how many times the rod rips off after only being cast out for just a few minutes.

Pop ups are an effective tactic in the angler's armoury, used correctly they can be the difference between a fish on the bank or experiencing a blank session. Carp are curious creatures, they have no hands to touch objects in their path and they will use their mouths to investigate items that remotely look like food. They also have the added advantage of being buoyant and counter balanced with putty, will be easier for a carp to suck up the other baits. Don't think of the pop up as a chuck it and chance it tactic, it can be deadly in the right situation.

Printed in Great Britain
by Amazon